A Waterfall of Words

A Waterfall of Words

Palmyra M. Williams

Canadian Cataloguing in Publication Data

Williams, P.M.(Palmyra Mary),1937-
a waterfall of words
Poems,

I. Title
PS8595.156275W37 1999C811' .54C98-911217-9
PR9199.3. W4916W37 1999

228-151-10090, 152nd Street
Surrey BC.
Email: palwilly@yahoo.com
Ph# 604 584 9612

ISBN 0-9683509-3-3

A Waterfall of Words

Table of Contents

Foreword

As I listened in awed wonder
to the singing of the birds
I requested inspiration
Here's a varied presentation
of reflections
In this waterfall
of words

Acknowledgments

Many thanks to my sons J.C (Chris) Philip, Wayde, my Daughter Vivienne, the late Gloria Crichlow, Ms. Vivienne Fisher, my writing circle for their help and constructive input. Mrs. Violet Haas. Jennifer Harland,
Williams. Terri Brice, And the late Anna Yen.

To my son J.C, Terri Brice, and The late Anna Yen

Realization

The race, must survive intact
I've got to be strong.
I'm tired, but I cannot give up
not yet, not yet
while the dilemma persist.
The universal cry of
the oppressed,
their heirs apparent
visible, yet invisible
misunderstood...misinterpreted.
Don't treat me this way.
Have a care,
I'm alone
needing a strong shoulder
to cry on, to lean on
but no one is there.
Enough,
enough my scions.
Stand
Stand up
on your own two feet
and claim your birthright.
I no longer have the ability
to put my shoulders to the wheel,
to forge a new path.
Not as much.
That torch is now yours
to carry and press on.

Establishment

Let me take a breath
a long deep breath
Let me feel the cool air
in my nostrils.
Let me see
the azure blue of the heavens,
the golden sun,
a passing flock of carefree birds
winging their way
across the cloudless sky
on a balmy day.
Who am I?
Where is my direction?
My location, my roots.
My sons and daughters
Look at me.
I am a megalith
and the embodiment of deep disquiet.
I am burdened by adversity and censure.
My very soul feels negation.
This must not,
cannot continue
There has to be a better way.

Commission

A discordant sound rings out
and echoes from deep
within the soul of the overwhelmed
a muffled agonized plea is expressed.
Help us, please,
we feel so helpless.
Give us assistance
Give us inspiration and hope.
We are afraid of the unknown.
and have lost our sense of direction.
The answer is promptly returned.
Help yourself.
Open your eyes look around you
and look within yourself
there you will find your own solutions.
Face your personal demons
and try to overcome them
If you truly believe you'll triumph
then you will do so.
Along the way, sing a song.
Sing a euphoric song of joy
and take delight
in the rhythms, the lilts
and the beautiful cadences.
For you are a child of the universe
Reclaim your intensity,
your dignity
your heritage
your history.
And your sense of purpose
Your children need you
now more than ever
to recapture their nobility.

Verbose soliloquy on Contrapuntal Music
By a beleaguered first year music student

Oh, confounded counterpoint
thou hast the ability to incapacitate
the mental faculties of the entity
Could thy name be malice?
Since maleficence appears thy quest?
Creator Benign
whether be the prevailing entity
whose intellectual processes
so deviously sinister,
so cunningly and strategically
labyrinthine that it attempts
to ensnare,
psychoanalyze and codify
a nondescript conception of egos
long since dissipated?
Consequently
creating a frangibility of
the plebeian consciousness.
This... coupled with
a chaotic panoply of unstable directions
variegated
in its multifarious facets
obtuse intricate character and
dubious consistency.
By it's very configurations,
tragically reduces the unwary
or the inquisitive who question its validity,
to a state
of intense
ego demoralization
and uncertainty,

combined with
a case of severe cerebral diversion
entitial mento- plastic
porosity
or spasticity,
whichever condition initiates priority soonest.
Combobulatory security
hastily dissipates,
leaving in its wake
flabbergasted indifference,
which now boldly stalks
the seeming vacuous corridors
Of consciousness.
A distressing consternation
overtakes
the reality of the ego's
obvious attempted destruction.
Which
 now reacting in panic
 at the rapidly approaching
 unaccustomed mental turmoil,
evident impending fractured rationality
and seeming decline of instinctive positivity,
recoils,
at the likely onset
of its clearly looming
mercurial mental catastrophes,
and quizzically undertakes to query itself,
the universe in general
Its specific location
in relation to everything else,
reason for existence
and its intended purpose in life.
Oh,
perfidiously
contrapuntal
codificatory meanders,

release thy
 incomprehensible grasp
 on innocently fastidious souls.
Thy malevolent tentacles
challenge psychological stability.
Thy doubtful theoretical insincerity
confounds the erudite
and condemns the undergraduate
to a state of quivering insecurity.
Thou infant of a Machiavellian intuition
banish thyself to infinite spherification.

Welcome to Life .Class 101

Fascination, Expectation
Deliberation, Demonstration
Consideration, Concentration
Experimentation, Application
Confrontation, Intimidation
Consternation, Desperation
Examination, Desolation
Demoralization, Humiliation
Commiseration, Identification
Verification, Justification
Validation, Amelioration
 Consolation, Presentation
Vindication, Exoneration
Exhilaration, Satisfaction
Gratification, Commendation
Convocation
Congratulations

Ebonium

Oh, Beleaguered Woman
put away the hammer
It has served its purpose.
Replace it with the velvet glove
Accept positivity and repel negativity.
Look within you and discover
your vitality and your beauty,
that's where you've buried it
Be gentle
because gentility becomes you
Smile, it makes you glow.
Walk tall now, lift up your chin.
Then, your sons and daughters
will see your comeliness
and revere you.
You have come so far,
now go farther
You have climbed
the emotional mountains.
It is time to rejoice
in the green valleys,
the lush vales
and the peaceful dells.
Sit awhile
Take time to lazily ponder
beneath a tree
to dream once again.
It was not always thus
Return again to the land of wonder.
Sit by a stream and become
who you were meant to be.
Breathe . . .
Relax . . .Enjoy.

Why?

The curious child asks
Why does my hair defy gravity?
Why is there such a beautiful range
of colors of the skin
from ecru to ebony?
with textures from silk to velvet
My skin looks like crushed velvet
so soft and warm.
The soles of my feet
and the palms of my hands
demand explanations
Why are they lighter in color?
You. ..
my scion
are a descendant
of the Ebony Environs
of the Nile.

Envy

Jealousy.
A lethal poison Lurking
in the dark passages of the mind
It denigrates, decimates
Deviates and abominates
It devalues, discredits
Divides, and distorts
It disparages, dehumanizes
Destabilizes, and destroys
It degrades, defiles
Disfigures, and dissipates
It debilitates, depreciates
Disgusts, and diminishes
It suppurates, victimizes
Vandalizes, and violates
It is negative, vindictive
Reactive and destructive
It is Brutal, Terrifying
Fanatical, and Demonizing

Preoccupation

I am ...
I'm on a roll,
Don't stop me now,
Don't block my path either.
I am on a journey of self discovery,
And a quest for knowledge
in all its shapes disguises and forms.
Each day
There's a new lesson to be learnt,
new things to discover.
Amusement, apprehension
animosity,
ecstasy
and all the ramifications
of living a life
to its utmost presentations,
Challenges, predicament
and illuminations.
Come with me,
let us learn together.
Don't stop me but
Don't hold me back either
Or I'll perchance be constrained
unwillingly
to leave you behind
in the momentum
and in the unrelenting and persistent
compulsion
for spiritual
and physical evolution

Parade of the Dispossessed

It was a fine sunny Sunday
and that special time
when everyone enjoyed
the tranquility of a cool quiet clime
I looked out the window in carefree delight
when a strangely odd spectacle came into sight.
First one person passed by.
He looked strangely smeared
Then ever so slowly
more strangers appeared
A trickle of persons
grew into a crowd,
the bizarre apparition
made me call out aloud
In fear and foreboding, I started to cry
And yelled for my parents who were resting nearby
They rushed to the window
to witness the scene
of an endless parade of marchers strangely serene.

Many witnessing bystanders started to cry
in alarm and in sorrow on seeing them go by.
Men and women walked slowly
on aged shuffling feet
Some were limping,
on crutches, or in basket chair seats
The pathetic procession beat a steady retreat
to the ominous rhythm of travel weary feet.
Not a sound passed their lips
as they passed out of sight
They were dressed very simply
and seemed aghast at their plight

Neither one nor the other
even looked left
or right
Could this human misery ever be right?
A ripple of horrified questions rang out,
I declare . . .
From the sidewalk onlookers
who were watching in fear
One curious onlooker
Stepped out of the crowd
he wanted to know.
He was talking quite loud.
'Excuse me . . . mister',
he said
'What's all this about
Can you tell me the reason
You've chosen this route?
In the good name of God man,
What on earth have you done
to experience such calamity of magnitude one?'
We'd all like to know
if our turn will be next
Do we have to prepare
is there hidden pretext?
Where are the young ones?
There are none in the group?
Where are the children?
there's not one in your troupe?'
A tired head lifted,
despair etched in the face
We're the members,
He said.
Of a discounted race
When with youth on our side
our strength there to abuse,
we were welcomed
to fight in our country of choice.

We're much too old now.
We're a politic excuse.
By the country we helped build
and worked to defend
since we never were citizens
this thanks is our end
We... now the aged,
now more of a threat.
We're of no further of use.
We've placed the lost bet.
We're now the discarded,
predisposed to misuse,
no longer the aces,
We're just simply ...
The duce.
Our possessions were pilfered,
our identities gone
Our talents
forgotten,
we've been told to move on.
Our homes confiscated,
all our funds suddenly obscured.
Then brutally deported
 to a strange island's shore
His weary brow crinkled,
a tear spilled down his cheek.
His eyes sadly dropped.
He was too choked up to speak.
The uncalled for disgrace
 made his shoulders droop low
 as his soft voice continued,
 I've a distance to go
Nightfall's fast approaching,
the dark soon will be here
I've no place to call home yet,
must get going I fear.
Please excuse my bad manners

I have to move on, 'fore the dark evening comes
before daylight is gone.
I have to keep going to find me some home
My trek's not yet over,
my march must go on.
I'll never ever forget
that fine sunny day
a regime's brutal practice,
marred my childhood that day,
as the Parade of the Dispossessed
happened my way.

Braggadocios Domain

Is invariably
Vainglorious with vaunting visions
Pompous with petulant peeves
Highfalutin with hectic hinting
Pretentious with puffed up proposals
Grandiose with guarded guile
Cheeky with chuckling cheerfulness
Boastful with blissful blemishes
Bombastic with blistering blunders
And Resolute with risky reasoning.

Creative Materialization

Imagination visualization,
Illumination exploration.
Inception formulation
Speculation, calculation, embarkation.
Experimentation, documentation
Classification, implementation
Frustration
Illustration, adaptation, rectification
Application, augmentation, replication
Revelation
Determination, demonstration. Dissertation
Declaration.
Conversation, Rationalization, investigation
Justification.
Examination, evaluation, corroboration
Reproduction.
Certification registration
Elucidation presentation
Recommendation
Proposition, publication,
Exposition
Nomination exhibition
Intensification remuneration
Lionization
Celebration.

Ageism

The philosophy of aging
 is one propagated by elements
 of insecurity, fear and inability
 to accept the universe
 as the great coordinator of all things.
The spirit never ages.
Just the thought processes
 of the individual thinker.

Wordorama

Waffling with words,
Nibbling at nothingness
Feasting on foibles
Tampering with truth
Tinkering with trivialities
The trappings of travesty
Tyranny of trends
Tournaments of intolerance

Plethora of platitudes

Pointlessly parochial
Pivotally poised
Pretentiously precise
Pettifogginly pestiferous
Pathologically picayune
Salaciously sinful
Puritanically pompous
Pleasingly playful
Bubblingly   bilious
Ploddingly persistent
Palpably ponderous
Fundamentally fixated
Tediously temperate
Spectacularly specious
Tactfully taciturn
Tabulatingly tentative
Writhingly rhthymnic.

Fear.

A crippling emotion
which paralyzes
and encompasses
the audacity and fervor of a life
in a grasp like that of an iron band.
None is immune.
Determined efforts however
can be made to break its fetters
but it never leaves completely.
Continually lurking,
in the recesses of the mind
awaiting an opportunity
of inattention
to return at a moments notice
and enervate its hapless victims.

Lottery windfall

The emotional intoxication of
Jubilatory disbelief,
Ecstatic tipsification
Elective acquisition
Electrifying incredulity
Unrestrained exuberation
Vociferous exclamation
Indisputable registration
Rejuvenation
Invigorative transformations
Speculative elaboration
Expansive transactions
Redecorative ornamentations
Locomotive titilations
Sophisticated designations
Administrative captivations, and
Luxurious relocations.

Estrangement

Disillusion, Insulation,
Agitation distortion,
Disapproval
Cynicism, skepticism.
Indiscretion
Alienation, disintegration
Dispossession, separation
Devastation.
Alienation, dissolution.
Pessimistic devastation.
Acceptance.
Detachment.

Words to a daughter on her Wedding day.

My precious daughter,
from the very first moment I met you
I fell in love with you
and that love has never waivered.
I have always considered you
my personal gift from God.
I thank you
for choosing to come into my life
and allowing me the joy
of being your mother,
and I thank God
for his wonderful gift
of a daughter.

Once upon a time

The old school house
was weathered and broken.
The old school mistress' posture
was now bent low.
She had seen better days.
Her face was now lined,
and with graying hair.
She sat quietly reminiscing,
a small lone figure on one of
the creaking benches
still barely intact
but
now worn quite smooth with time.
Here, children once learned
to read and pray,
laughed and cried.
The old school yard
was strangely silent and deserted.
The last school child long gone,
The once beaten path to the old school house doors
were covered with leaves and ferns
No longer, children's voices calling,
squeals of laughter, angry screams,
or howls of pain and childish rage,
Just the old school mistress
With her memories, sitting there
all alone.
Quietly.
Looking far away
thinking of another time,
and recalling what once was.

The Conference

I must not forget the date.
This ticket cost me a bundle so
I can't afford to let the occasion
carelessly pass by.
The time has arrived so quickly.
Its time to find that elusive location
and secure parking
where I won't get towed away.
Ah! Here's a good spot.
Oh no! Parking fees.
Still, not too far from the entrance
I've got my ticket . . . good.
Excuse me?
Did you say I can't park here?
I've already bought a ticket
Can it be transferred
to the other location?
Oh my!
Well, here I go again.
Haven't even begun
and I'm already out three extra dollars.
This is not good
I'll try this parking lot
Can this ticket be validated?
I paid at the other lot
In front of the building
I really have to buy another one?
Fine way to start the day.
I hope this is not an indication
of the direction
of the rest of the conference.
This had better be worth it.
It had better be good.

The Peoples Princess

Never did the sun shine as brightly
Never had the world watched as sadly
Never had the country suffered such pain
Never had the city seen such communal anguish
Never did the old town smell as sweet and
Never before were the streets of the old city
covered in such an array of flowers
in expansive abundance
colour and beauty
imparting peace
around the buildings
walkways and thoroughfares
Never before had the people
cried out in such sorrow and
such sense of deep loss
in such a unanimous vocalization
of bereavement
as on the day of the funeral of Diana,
the People's Princess.

Unnecessary Wordification?

In high school I came across a poem. I liked it
It was wordy.
In fact it was used as an example
of the possible verbosity of a well known poem
I liked it in its entirety anyway,
The sole purpose for the creation of words
is for them to be used at will.
I love words.
The first stanza of that poem.
I remembered.

Scintillate Scintillate, globule vivific
Fain could I essay thy nature specific
Vaulting poised in the ether portentous
Skillfully resembling a gem carbonaceous.
THAT'S IT! Wonderful, isn't it?

Pensively Painted Poems

Waterfalls Fountains Geysers Streams
Rivers Rivulets Lakes and Ponds
Oceans, Seas, all watery arenas
alive with a myriad explosion
of pictorial life forms.
Wavelets gently lapping
on the golden sands
of the sea shore
on a sunny summers day
Love truth and beauty attesting to
The omnipresent
magnificence of being.
Shadows and dreams
Colour and fragrance
attracting passionate emotions
Glens leas and meadows
Pastures forests, vales and dells
Deserts, Jungles, mountains plains
Peaks and valleys
Ribbons of road
Whiter the white
Bluer than blue
Newer than new
Reflective meditation.

A Planet Unexcelled

Its character was like that of a big blue marble
in its lonely rotational orbit.
The topography suggested application
of intense creative thought
with flora and fauna sensationally verdant
lush and vibrant abounded.
in an unbelievable plethora
of colours, shapes, sizes and complexities
from the extraordinary
to the unexpected
all producing a variety of provisions
for individual nutrition,
and entertainment
in structured hues, aromas,
and sensitivities
to titillate,
entice and satiate
the five senses
of every occupant
inhabiting its opportune dimensions .

The surface seemed extraordinarily alluring
and exhilarating.
Large bodies of water
covering much of the planet's crust
appeared to sparkle in delight
as the golden rays of sunshine
danced upon its silvery surface,
during the daylight hours.
Twinkling, as if alive with the sheer joy of creation,
and completely aware of themselves.

Beneath the seemingly innocuous watery façade,
unheard of multiplicity of marine beings flourished,
from the denizens of the deep,
to the occupants of the clear shoals.
Life everywhere,
swimming, diving, living and dying,
according to a natural order.
Their apparent carefree joy
physical, beauty
and grace attested to their adaptation
of this matchless milieu as they
glided through their watery medium
with effortless speed and grace.
Again, from the microscopic to the mammoth
inhabiting this mysterious world

In all places,
water moved over and under the landscape,
exploding, upward and outward
as if in an unspoken eagerness
in the most unlikely and pristine scenarios
traversing the land with only one aim,
to reach the sea by all possible means
and overflowing
with abundant,
curious and inquisitive life.

Oceans, seas, lakes, pools, ponds,
creeks, rivers, rivulets, streams springs
All busily flowing splashing, trickling, rippling,
meandering, and persuing their affairs
as if on a irresolute deadline with infinity,
The miniscule
to the majestic.

The landscape
encompassed a scenic panorama of mountains,
valleys, hills, hillocks, cliffs, crags, dells,
Vales, ravines, plains desserts
and meadows,
representing an astonishing diversity of
life forms specific to each particular environment.
Each region, seemed to possess
its own sense of understanding.

The sensational act
was repeated in the inhabitants of the air.
Creatures of flight of every pattern, hue, and attitude
traversed the azure blue skies.
There was the array of aerial wildlife.
From the majesty of the Great eagle
to the intense, yet orderly activity
of the hummingbird
existing, in symbiosis.
The specie selection inconceivable
within every framework,
thriving, in apparent joy and great ease
reveling in the legacy of freedom.

The creatures of the air were
all cunningly crafted to utilize
their environment to the utmost possibility,
soaring on air currents to conserve energy,
they possessed the added ability
to orientate themselves to their position
in relation to the air above
and the land below
wherever and whenever
they chose,
for optimum advantage.
Every known and unknown method of transportation
were utilized to its best advantage.

Excellent visual perception was a boon
for self-preservation and nourishment.

On the dry land
the diversity of each life form was honoured
and just as well deliberated
Each design
was as unique and beautiful as its predecessor
From the miniature to the enormous,
this was indeed the architectural design
of an inexhaustible mind

every detail appeared to have been
carefully considered.
In the creation of this utopian world
Everything was evidently resolute
Nothing was left to chance
The vegetation was kept well watered by rainfall
The result of evaporation and condensation
From the myriad bodies of water
Air currents cooled the air
and cleared it of pollutants and irritants.

The oceans were kept habitable
By the constantly churning wave activity
And the ebb and flow of tidal movement.
The action of the sun's rays
Encouraged vegetative growth
And further production of variegated life
The land cleansed it self, sometimes casually,
And sometimes with controlled violence

As if on an ordered agenda,
volcanic activity and earthquakes
periodically transforming the landscape

Deconstructing and rebuilding
moving and changing
and occasional gale force winds
cleared away the atmospheric debris
of creation in progress

Temperature variation was organized
into zones
Tropic and sub-tropic
Temperate and sub-temperate
From cold to very cold
Warm to hot
Indeed a palette for every taste
And persuasion

The land itself
Held incredible secrets
Below it's surface
In the forms of metals, ores, crystals
And wonderful surprises in mines
caves coves and crevasses.
This then . . . was Eden

Today

Today,
I will attempt
to weigh the difference as I perceive it
between
fact and fiction
truth and falsehood
success and failure
with tentative and believable
credulity

Sunshine

Sunshine,
sparkling on the water's surface
like diamonds,
enticing the curious,
beckoning the tentative,
and daring the courageous
to enter and enjoy.

Moonlight

 Reflecting
off the waters' shimmering surface at night
like the bold daub of yellow
by a painter's brush
on black oilskin.
Sinister.
Ominous
Menacing.

Silence

Be very still.
Listen.
Make peace within
and that peace
will spread like a stone
carelessly tossed
into a limpid pool,
sending ripples in all directions

Gratitude

Thanks
For a sound mind
in a healthy body
For freedom from pain
For a beautiful sunny day
For the knowledge
that everything progresses
in nature
as it should
without my conscious input
And.. most of all,
Thanks
For the spirit of patience, wisdom
and understanding,

Anguish

Last night my son, I feared you'd died.
You were only eight years old
I'd never thought it possible to suffer
such dreadful dereliction in my entire existence.
Such an overwhelming sensation of futility
that left me feeling like a weak empty carcase,
Like an onion ring. A hollow broken shell.
I was inconsolable and forlorn.
My heart was broken and shattered.
even though I was fully aware
that death was only a transition
to a higher state of being
desolation of spirit surrounded me.
Your brother and sister
made futile attempts to comfort me
by recapturing the many events,
wonderful memories,
good times the fun times
your entertaining remarks,
loving ways.
Inquisitive and impish ways
Your beautiful large hazel eyes
and your bewitching infectious smile.
Together, we recalled
the moments
of your tireless energetic and hair-raising escapades
and the joy and love you brought into our lives
in your short time spent with us.
I cradled your lifeless little body in my arms,
Still I could find no comfort in my grief
As I desperately attempted
to grasp at every faint hope

to forcefully will you back
to the land of the living.
My weary heart
felt like a cold nugget of lead
there is a profound void
where my heart used to be
in the very core of my being, a void which
could never again to be filled.
Thankfully, it was only a dream.
What a joy to know it was only a dream.
Nevertheless,
long after I had awaken from that dream
The residual emotion was so intense,
That the leaden feeling persisted
and dissipated as lethargically
as heavy fog on a chilly morning in November.
Amazingly, I had experienced
the full experience of the distress involved
as a result of the loss of a child
without the physical reality of such an occurrence
A all encompassing emotion
which cannot be described,
realized, or personally appreciated.
The stricken anguish,
The pain, hopelessness and helplessness
of a parent, who has just lost a child to death.

Control

To do the things,
I want to do.
To hear the things
I want to hear
On my own turf
In my own way
In my own time
I'll have my say.
In a manner I consider
magnificently my own
and at my own pace.
Unfettered,
by the intrinsic beliefs,
statistics, attitudes
dogma or philosophies
of persona from the past,
present or future.
I stand alone
in my own universe.
Accountable to no other
but my Creator and myself.

Art

What is art?

Art is the unlimited universal memorandum, unbounded by the aesthetic

Yet enclosing anything, everything and everyone everywhere.

Art is non-authoritative indefinable by none.

Neither is it in the exclusive domain of the so-called privileged.

No one entity is an expert on art, since it is created by both the enlightened and the illiterate.

The logical and illogical, the inanimate and animate.

Any adjustment a creature in nature willingly or unwittingly

chooses to document in life, is an art form.

There is no metre rule or ethic,

which can truly unequivocally state or determine good or bad art,

as is often demonstrated by the varied attempts of

the puffed up proclamations of floundering egos

in self- imposed and fruitless attitudes of pointless censure

As they unproductively proclaim themselves

guardians of general morality for the masses

and the sole experts on the subject of art.

Art appeals to a myriad of persons in all-encompassing sensibilities.

No hard and fast manipulation or wisdom can define this insight and

No true rule of thumb, liberality of thought or egotistical direction can evaluate.

Art is what it is, for what it is. Whether it is perceived as good or bad

Pure, polluted, noble or undisciplined, Abstract or directed,
    Discerning or unsavoury, Appealing or nauseating, Art
    is what it is for itself and of itself,
with apologies to no one. It is an expression of the soul.

Music

The melody of the spheres
The sound of the universe
The sounds of life
The songs of eternity
The critical song of existence
The alpha, and omega,
of are, am, is, and be.
All that is
All that is to come

All that will be
Music heralds the beginning of life,
the end of life
Mathematically, moving,
Powerfully majestic,
Pathetically, sombre,
Emotionally, sedate,
Disruptively, disturbing,
Unnerving.
Unexplainably undefined,
Unfathomably, unfettered.
Diabolically exciting,.
Serenely Angelic,
Exhilarating.

Petulance

Why do I have to stay here?
Standing in this place
like a cardboard cut-out
is driving me to distraction
I am a human being.
My knees can attest to that reality.
How come, I've never noticed knees before ?
When I was younger.
Now-a-days, knees, legs and feet
seem to occupy a great deal
of my waking time.
Old age, I am told,
has much to account
for the particular fixation
of this discomfiting affliction.
I CATEGORICALLY RESIST.
How dare my feet hurt?
To the best of my knowledge
I have not abused them.
Systems fail - of that I'm aware
but what has that got to do with me?
I never ran around willy-nilly in my youth.
Like many brave souls
who in an effort
to keep maintain good health
Pounded their knees into the ground
Running for no reason.
Indeed this is a horrible joke on me, since
walking . . .was my most dangerous sport.
JUST THAT-WALKING

Marriage

Until you have done
whatever you've always dreamed to do
gone wherever you've always wanted to go
seen whatever you've always hoped to see
Not until then my child
should you consider marriage.
Because marriage. . .
Is the period
at the end of a long sentence.

The Gift

She was very old woman
barely able to walk unaided
and considered by all of her colleagues
to be a grouch without par.
Somehow,
we formed a bond of friendship
and I sensed a kindred spirit.
She allowed me to lend her a hand
with her daily routines
as she determinedly struggled against
her ever-encroaching physical limitations.
One day without warning,
she presented me with a gift of a small orange
and in spite of my refusals she insisted that I accept it.
This to me was a offering of great significance
Because I knew it was her one special treat of the day,
and a fruit she really loved and enjoyed
during her tranquil times.
In offering me this fruit
she demonstrated the love of the universe in action.
And I felt honoured and totally inspired.

September 11th

Yesterday two planes filled with travelers
were deliberately set on a collision path
 to crash into two sky scrapers.
The twin structures had taken
many months to erect,
and considered by everyone
involved in its creation.
An edifice dedicated
as a symbol of peaceful interaction
between nations and invincible in the face of any disaster
was demolished in as many minutes.
And many lives were lost.
Fanatical assailants
with serious disrespect for life
claimed responsibility.
Barely had the dust settled than cries of vengeance rang
        out.
The anguished cries of the victims relatives,
and persons in positions of leadership
rallied for retribution.
They all cried tears of grief and desolation
The voices of reason were temporarily stilled.
The cycle of violence must be destroyed
that the cycle of hostility must be stopped
and each awake to the understanding
that comprehensive resolutions may
surface only when all responsible leaders
meet face to face
with honest expectations
and genuine respect
for each others customs, cultures and traditions
as equals,

with no reservations
accepting the knowledge
that all groups are harmed
by inaccurate or ignorant perceptions.
It is time for appeasement
Time to sit and talk to each other
and not at each other
in a spirit of understanding.
without ulterior motives
until everyone's voice is husky,
then send in like –minded replacements to talk
ad finitum until a truly honourable consensus
can be unanimously achieved.
Only then will the light at the end of the tunnel
be plainly visible,
the possibility of blinders of bias and mistrust lifting
the implied wrongs and misunderstandings
clarified, identified and deplored
and sincere apologies to all concerned
offered in a spirit of true goodwill and compassion
Maybe then fanaticism might lose its validation
and violence cease to be an appropriate avenue for
        attention
Instead its ineffectiveness may provide
 the incentive for all involved
to beat their weapons
into ploughshares.

Love

Love me dearly
As you should
With a love few mortals could
Put your outstretched hand in mine
Love divine
Love me truly
Soon we'll part
Only love can fill this heart
Hearts entwined
For all time
Love Divine

Summer

In summertime
I love to sit
In my cottage dimly lit.
The pleasing smell
of new mown hay
Strongly reminiscent
of those wonderful lazy hazy days
in summertime

Broad-spectrum

Love is like the explosion of a beautiful
bouquet of fragrant flowers
in the garden of the heart.
Time is like a swiftly passing
rain cloud on a hot summers day.
The mountains are like giant sentinels
standing at the gates of eternity.
Peace is a paradigm
In the postulation of the perceiver.

Collage

Hot, as a sun baked tarmac
Frightening as facing your most inner thoughts
High as a free falling parachutist
Powerful as a blast of icy winter wind
Lonely as the last rose of summer
Free as a babbling brook wending its way to the sea
Wet as a weeping willow
Funny as a dancing seal on stilts
Cold as the cunning in an enemy's heart
Sexy as the dance of the seven veils
Wind rippled water wrinkled as a slept on sheet
Tired as a giant sloth.
Sneaky as a slinky toy.

Mini Vocabulary

Mini vocabulary regarding some of the words used in Verbose Soliloquy

Counterpoint ...	Early fourth century music notation
Maleficience ...	Spitefulness, vindictiveness
Labyrinthine ...	Twisted
Frangibility ...	Weakness / mental insecurity
Plebian ...	Novice
Multifarious ...	Multiplicity
Entitial ...	Deep seated. Ingrained
Mento-plastic porosity. ..	Complete failure of normal analytical Primal fears. brain fatigue
Combobulatory ...	Self-confidence / self assurance.
Mercurial mental cathastrophe ...	Sudden cascade of irrational emotions
Contrapuntal ...	Relating to theoretical counterpoint
Codificatory meander ...	Uncipherable. , unpredictable
Malevolent ...	Evil
Machiavelli ...	A very astute European politician of ancient times
Spherification ...	Space

Biography

Palmyra has always written poetry for as long as she has been able to write. She often used this venue as a form of healing catharsis in any situation of life she considered stressful or overwhelming. It was only later in life, once her children had grown up and left home, and with much encouragement by friends and acquaintances, that she decided to consider publication of her works. Also among her repertoire are two self published memoirs titled,

"Say You Say Me." And
"The Mountains Eh? Dream On!"